Communities at Work™

Who's Who
in an
Urban Community

Jake Miller

The Rosen Publishing Group's
PowerKids Press™
New York

Published in 2005 by The Rosen Publishing Group, Inc.
29 East 21st Street, New York, NY 10010

First Edition

Editor: Joanne Randolph
Book Design: Maria E. Melendez
Layout Design: Emily Muschinske

Photo Credits: Cover and title page © Philip Gould/Corbis; p. 5 © Alan Schein Photography/Corbis; p. 7 © Jeffrey W. Myers/Corbis; p. 9 © Ariel Skelley/Corbis; p. 11 © Patricia Barry Levy/Index Stock Imagery; p. 13 © Roger Ressmeyer/Corbis; p. 15 © Jose Luis Pelaez, Inc./Corbis; p. 17 © Joel W. Rogers/Corbis; p. 19 © Jonathan Blair/Corbis; p. 21 © Paul Barton/Corbis.

Library of Congress Cataloging-in-Publication Data

Miller, Jake.
  Who's who in an urban community / Jake Miller.
       p. cm. — (Communities at work)
  Includes bibliographical references and index.
  ISBN 1-4042-2790-3 (library binding) — ISBN 1-4042-5034-4 (pbk.)
  1 Cities and towns—Juvenile literature. 2. Community life—Juvenile literature. 3. Metropolitan government—Juvenile literature. I. Title. II. Series.

  HT152.M55 2005
  307.76—dc22

                                        2004000489

Manufactured in the United States of America

Contents

Living and Working Together in a City

A **community** is a group of people who help each other get the things that they need and want. It is also the place in which these people live. Towns, cities, and neighborhoods are examples of communities. All the people who live, work, and play in a city are part of the **urban** community.

Cities are busy places where many people live and work together.

Growing Up in an Urban Community

Children who grow up in an urban community live with their families in houses and apartments in the city. They play with other children in their neighborhood. They go to the park and the playground. They buy snacks at the little store on the corner. They go to the zoo to see animals. They go to **museums** to learn about history, nature, and art.

Children who live in the neighborhood go to the playground to meet their friends and have fun.

Businesses Big and Small

There are many businesses in the urban community. They offer **goods** and **services** for the people who live there. The chief **executive** is the boss of a company. He or she is in charge of deciding what the company will make. He or she decides how the company will sell its goods and services.

This business owner works with the cook to serve food to people in the urban community. In an urban community, there are many different businesses that offer people the things that they need and want.

The City Council

Many urban communities have a city **council**. People in each neighborhood **elect** a city council member. The city councillors vote on new rules and laws for the city. They decide how much money the city **government** can spend. They decide what to spend the money on.

Each neighborhood picks its own city council member. This way every neighborhood has a voice in what happens in its urban community.

The Mayor

The mayor is the leader of the urban community. He or she runs the city government. The mayor makes sure the city streets get cleaned. He or she makes sure the people are safe from crime. The mayor helps the urban community to run smoothly.

The mayor is the person in charge of the whole city government. San Francisco mayor Dianne Feinstein was the first woman to be elected as mayor of that city. She served from 1978 to 1988.

The Judge

The judge is an important member of the urban community. The judge explains rules and laws. The judge's job is to decide if a person has broken the law. The judge also has to decide what should be done to someone who breaks the law.

A judge helps make sure that the people living in the urban community are safe and are treated fairly.

Even though people love the fun of the city, it is important to have a quiet place to rest and play. Parks and gardens give people in the city a place to feel like they are a part of nature.

Keeping the City Green

There are places that all the people in the urban community share. Public gardens are one such place.

The gardeners who work in the garden take care of all the plants that grow there. They make the urban community a nice place to live.

Gardeners in public gardens grow many different kinds of flowers. Some even grow fruits and vegetables to eat!

At the Museum

A museum **curator** is part of the urban community. The curator is in charge of what the museum shows. The **exhibits** at the city museum tell the story of the community. They show the different kinds of art that artists in the city have made over the years. They show the way people used to live in the city's neighborhoods.

Many city museums have exhibits that are fun. These children are learning about dinosaur remains that were found near their city.

Urban Planning

In urban communities many people share a small space. An urban planner helps the city decide the best way to use the space that it has. A city may decide it wants a new highway or a new park. Urban planners find the best place to build these things.

Urban planners help the city to make good use of its space. They also try to make the city look nice for the people who live there.

Life in the City

In a big city, there are many different kinds of people. Some work right in the neighborhood where they live. Some live in towns outside the city and only come to the city to work. Some drive and some take the bus. Some speak different languages and wear different kinds of clothes. They are all part of the urban community.

Glossary

community (kuh-MYOO-nih-tee) A place where people live and work together, or the people who make up such a place.

council (KOWN-sul) A group called together to discuss or settle questions.

curator (KYUR-ay-tuhr) A person who puts on shows and controls collections at a museum.

elect (ee-LEKT) To pick for a job.

executive (eg-ZEK-yoo-tiv) The chief or boss of a company or other group.

exhibits (ig-ZIH-bits) Public shows at a museum.

goods (GUDZ) Things that people can buy and sell.

government (GUH-vern-mint) The people who make laws and run a state or a country.

museums (myoo-ZEE-umz) Places where art or historical articles are safely kept for people to see and study.

services (SER-vis-ez) Things that people do to or for other people.

urban (UR-bun) Having to do with a city.

Index

Web Sites

Due to the changing nature of Internet links, PowerKids Press has developed an online list of Web sites related to the subject of this book. This site is updated regularly. Please use this link to access the list: www.powerkidslinks.com/caw/whourban/